Upsherin

Exploring the Laws, Customs & Meanings of a Boy's First Haircut

Rabbi DovBer Pinson

Brooklyn, New York

Published for Iyyun by Ben Yehuda Press
430 Kensington Road
Teaneck, NJ 07666
http://www.BenYehudaPress.com

Iyyun Center for Jewish Spirituality
232 Bergen St
Brooklyn NY 11217
Contact@Iyyun.com
http://www.Iyyun.com

Library of Congress Cataloging-in-Publication Data

Pinson, DovBer, 1971-
Upsherin : exploring the laws, customs & meanings of a boy's first haircut / DovBer Pinson.
p. cm.
ISBN 978-1-934730-33-1
1. Upsheren. 2. Hair—Religious aspects—Judaism. I. Title.
BM720.U57P56 2010
296.4'42—dc22
2010019852

pb ISBN13 978-1-934730-33-1

10 11 12 / 10 9 8 7 6 5 4 3 2 1

Dedication

Many thanks to Gershon (Gregory) and Chanie Bell.
May their support for Torah be a source of blessings for them and their entire family.

To clarity, Emunah and Bitachon

May Hashem bless them with material and spiritual success, and give them the Koach to go "from strength to strength" in Avodas Hashem.

Contents

Upsherin

Upsherin

There is a custom that has been practiced by many Jews throughout the entire world for generations, a ceremony celebrating a boy's first haircut. The primary purpose of the haircut is to reveal the *peyos*/side locks. Shortly, we will explore the relevance of *peyos*.

The Yiddish name for this ceremony is *Upsherin*, a phrase that comes from the German word *sheren*/shear and *auf*/off. In Hebrew, this ceremony is called *Tisporet*.

While not based on any Talmudic teaching, the custom to celebrate a boy's first haircut has been around for hundreds of years. A student of R. Yitzchak Luria (1534-1572) writes that his teacher took his family to the gravesite of the 1st century sage, R. Shimon bar Yochai. There he performed his young son's first haircut with great joy and festivity, "according to the well-known tradition". This event took place on the 33rd day of the counting of the *Omer*, a day which also marks the passing of R. Shimon Bar Yochai.

In the Torah, we find that *Avraham*/Abraham "made a great feast the same day that *Yitzchak*/Isaac was weaned" (*Bereishis* 21:8). The great 11th century commentator, R. Shlomo Yitzchaki, otherwise known as Rashi, wrote that this feast took place on Yitzchak's second birthday as he entered his third year of life. Perhaps this is in commemoration of a transitional moment in a child's maturation.

Clearly, a three-year-old boy undergoes a period of major transformation—the journey from babyhood to childhood. During this time, he moves from completely depending on the mother to functioning as an independent being.

This transition is somewhat related to the *Upsherin*. In earlier traditional sources, there is discussion as to when parents should give their boy his first haircut. One source advised the first shearing should take place as early as thirteen weeks; another, two years; and others explore the ripe old age of five. Often today, this celebration is held on the third birthday. Select Chassidic groups, however, perform the *Upsherin* on the boy's second birthday, upon his entering his third year of life.

In a beautiful metaphor, the child is the bounty of the parents, just as the fruit is the bounty of the trees. According to *Torah* law (*Vayikra* 19:23), we may not indulge in the fruit of trees within the first three years of their planting. This injunction is referred to as the laws of *orlah*, literally translated as "concealment." Similarly, the child's hair may be left uncut for the first three years of life.

The Idea of *Orlah*: Blocked Energy

The human/tree connection is employed often in the *Torah.* For example, "A person is like the tree of a field..." (*Devarim* 20:19). "For as the days of a tree, shall be the days of my people"(*Yeshaya* 65:22). "He will be like a tree planted near water..."(*Yirmiyhu* 17:8). In fact, our relationship with trees runs quite deep. Originally, mankind's sustenance came only from the fruit of the tree, as the Torah says, "And *Hashem* said, 'Of every tree of the garden you may freely eat'" (*Bereishis* 2:16). The implication is that mankind was invited only to eat the fruit of the tree, and not to partake of any other form of vegetation.

The connection between humans and trees was drawn based on our similarity. The tree grows in opposite directions. The outer, visible part of the sedling reaches upward towards the sun; whereas the inner, concealed roots burrow into the earth. We too grow physically upward and outward, while our spiritual growth turns inward. We give fruit as trees do; and the less dry a person is, the more pliable and gentle he becomes.

We will explore the relationship between the first three years of a human's life and the first three years of a tree's. But first let us turn to the meaning of *orlah.*

In the *Torah,* we find the term *orlah* used in reference to the first three years of fruit (*Vayikra* 19:23); with regard to the foreskin that is removed during circumcision (*Bereishis* 17:11); and in reference to removing the *orlah* from the heart (*Devarim* 10:16). In all three scenarios, *orlah* suggests a covering over, a blocking of something within.

In the case of the tree, the fruit remains closed to our participation or involvement. The fruit of the tree for the first three years remains outside of our human domain; we are forbidden to eat it. The energy within the fruit that gives us our nourishment remains concealed and removed from us. Similarly, removing the *orlah*/foreskin is an act of revealing; allegorically, it represents removing the outer layer of our hearts in order to reveal the deeper levels of self.

On a simple level, a little boy with long hair has *peyos*/sidelocks, but they are hidden. By means of the haircut, his *peyos* are now revealed. The difference between a pre-*Upsherin* state and a post-*Upsherin* state is that in the former state the *peyos* are intermingled with the head hair with no distinction between the hair on the head and the hair running down alongside the head. Through the *Upsherin*, an act of *havdalah*/separation is made. The importance of the process of distinguishing and making borders is integral to our mental and spiritual development. We will discuss this at greater length later.

The Age of Three: A Time of Transition

Every age, every movement of change is marked by a ceremony to show support for the one undergoing the transition, as well as to facilitate a smoother, less turbulent transition.

Children moving from what can be called a pre-personal stage to a personal stage, going from non-self awareness to self-awareness, become very protective of both their space and their ego. When a child first discovers his own separateness from the mother, that he is a distinct person with an individual body and has unique wants and desires, this awareness can be as frightening as it is empowering. The process of separation individuation, as some psychologists refer to it, begins at an early age of life, and shows up with a kind of vengeance in the second year of life, the terrible twos, as they are known.

When the child nears his third year of life, on a developmental level, he enters a transitional stage. No longer a baby swaddled in diapers drinking a bottle, he is now a boy. He emerges from the sheltered comfort of the home and steps out into school and is surrounded by friends in addition to his immediate family. Simply, the baby has matured and is beginning a new phase in growing up, from an insular protected life to one less sheltered. Similar to the fruit of the tree after its third year, the child's fruit, his personality, may now be shared and appreciated by others.

To mark this advancement into maturity and to make it memorable, an *Upsherin* is celebrated. With joy and various intriguing customs, this occasion is meant to excite the child, to infuse him with enthusiasm.

Three Stages of Child Development

To create the new, there needs to be a loosening of the old. Often, the first thing needed is a *havdalah*/radical break, separation from the past to move forward into a more rewarding future. A seed rots in the earth before it can offer new life; first comes sterility, then comes fertility.

On a developmental level, a child passes through three stages of transformation from birth until the age of three. Each stage requires its own *havdalah* so that later there can be greater *hamtakah*/sweetening and re-integration on a deeper, more profound level.

The first and principal *havdalah*/separation in the life of every living being is the process of birth itself. Birth occurs through a great *tzimtzum*/contraction that literally ejects a fetus from the comfort of her warm mother's womb. Immediately, a total, radical *havdalah* is needed in the form of cutting the umbilical cord, as the fetus severs ties with her mother. The *havdalah* of birth is so devastating to the mother, manifesting in the form of separation anxiety (some are very conscious of the experience, others less so), that the mother becomes *tamei*, translated as "impure," but implying a connection with death.

Ritual impurity of *Torah* law has nothing to do with hygiene or uncleanliness, rather it indicates a person's involvement or connection with the concept of death. The mother, having carried the fetus for nine or so months with the fetus being *yerech imo*/part and within the body of the mother herself, the birth of the child outside of the womb is a form of death. With the eventual severance of the umbilical cord, there is a drastic form of *havdalah*. This movement is overwhelming and devastating for all parties, from pre-birth *ibbur*/fetus status to post-birth *yenuka*/suckling status.

The next movement for the male child is from pre-*Bris*, an *aral* condition to post-*Bris*, a *mahul* condition, from pre-covenant reality to entering into the covenant of *Avraham*. For the first seven days of his life, the baby boy is pre-*Bris*. Only on the eighth day is the child given the opportunity, albeit by his parents 'decision, to enter into a transcendent, everlasting connection with his Creator.

Seven represents creation, the cycle of the week, duration of time, celebration of what is, and is reflected in the lower seven *sefiros*. Eight represents transcendence, that which is above the natural cycle of time and beyond the immediate, celebrating and anticipating what could be. The cutting, the *havdalah* of the *Bris* removes the *orlah*, the covering over, the foreskin, and reveals this transcendent eternal bond which can be felt and observed even in the physical body. The female child is born post-covenant and does not need a process to reveal the covenant, "*Isha k'man de'mahila dami*/A woman is like circumcised". Accordingly, women's bodies are innately fashioned to create anew, and bring life into this world; thus they are more naturally connected with transcendence.

Up until a certain age, children feel themselves bodiless, genderless even, much like *Adam* and *Chava* (Adam and Eve) before becoming aware of their nakedness. We all experience times, whether at the beginning of one's life or in the midst, when our lives mimic the life of Adam in the garden of the Tree of Life, when there is total oneness and integration, with no awareness of separation.

With regard to young children, when they this way, without shame and with a desire to be appreciated as they are, the challenge of parents or friends is to honor and give young children that space for them to just be, without a definition. For a boy to just be, without needing to be a "boy."

At each stage of the first three years, whenever there is monumental movement, there is a break with the old, a cutting off, *havdalah*/separation. From cutting the umbilical cord, moving from within mother to independence, to the *Bris*, to the *Upsherin*; now the little baby is a little boy.

From being a young genderless child, as it were, to becoming a boy at the age of three, parents begin to educate the child in the ways of a Torah observant boy. This is first done by cutting his head hair, leaving the *peyos* and putting on a *yarmulka*, otherwise known as a *kipa*/headcovering, and wearing *tzitzis*. The *Upsherin* expresses the child's becoming a boy, losing the girl hair and assuming a shorter, more defined boy haircut.

Boundless & Borders: Circles & Lines

Sa'ar is the Hebrew word for hair. The letters that make up the word for hair can also spell the word *sha'ar*/gate and *shi'ur*/measurement. Every separate strand of hair represents a measurement, a precise boundary, a particular gate.

In addition to the hair itself, the act of an *upsherin*, which creates the *peyos*, expresses even more so the idea of establishing a boundary and affirming a border. The word *peyos* is the plural form of the word *peah*, whose *gematria*/numerical value is 86 (*pei*/80, *aleph*/1, *hei*/5 = 86). This has the same *gematria* as the Divine name *Elokim* (*aleph*/1, *lamed*/30, *hei*/5, *yud*/10, *mem*/40= 86.) *Elokim* represents the aspect of din/judgment, boundary, order. The creation of the physical world is through *Elokim*, as in: "In the beginning, *Elokim* created..."

In the Torah, we find the idea of *peah* in reference to a field owner and the poor. Torah law requires that a person who owns a field leave some of the crop (rabbinically, at least one-sixtieth of the entire crop) for the poor. "When you reap the harvest of your land, you shall not reap to the very corners of your field... You shall leave them for the poor and stranger" (*Vayikra*. 19:9-10). Left at the edge and corner of the field, the *peah* itself sets up a boundary, a border that separates what the field owner gets for himself, and what the poor receive for themselves.

Dialectically speaking, the border of *peah* actually establishes a separation for the purpose of greater unification. By setting aside a portion for the poor within the field of an owner, a relationship between owner and the people who collect the produce is established, a relationship that would otherwise not necessarily exist. The border separates to allow for deeper connections.

The charity that is given from the more fortunate to the less fortunate establishes a relationship between giver and receiver. Ultimately, a deep bond between the two owners is revealed, the person who gives it away, and the person who now has it in his possession. *Tzedakah* is generally the Hebrew word used for charity, though literally translated, it means doing what is right. Clearly, there is a marked distinction between giving charity and doing what is right. To be charitable is to assume that the money or belongings are yours, that you are nice enough to give away your money or possessions to others. *Tzedakah* means doing right, being aware that the money you are giving to the poor has been offered to you as a gift, to be kept in your trust until you distribute it to its proper owner.

Suppose you own a field and set aside a *peah* on the corner of your field. A line is drawn exposing how much belongs to you, how much of yours is in fact yours, and what of yours belongs to others. The *peah* reveals how much of you *mispashet*/extends and spreads out over your own belongings, and where there is a clear divide, a distinct perimeter where the other begins.

Peyos/the corners of the hair, which are the sideburns or ear locks, serve the same purpose. *Peyos* on the field and on the hair both set a distinction, a border and simultaneously allow for a deeper connection between the head hair and eventual facial hair, between the child and the people around him.

Peyos are indistinguishable for the person who goes with long, unkempt hair. Long hair, as will shortly be explored, represents untamed, unbridled and unrestrained energy, energy that *mispashet*/extends non-restrictively in all directions and places, free flowing and wild. A small baby boy running about before his *Upsherin*, long hair flowing behind him, represents a little bundle of energy, brimming with life and exuberance. It is a beautiful thing for a young developing child to secure his ego and be wild. Yet it is a period of life with no borders or understanding of others. In these early years of life, the prime saying of the youngster is "It's mine" or "I want it."

Mimicking the cosmic process of creation, where initially came *tohu*/chaos then *tikun*/correction, a child, for the first few of years of life, functions in a reality of *tohu* on all levels of existence, both in a state of chaos as well as being the source of chaos for others.

The cosmic force of *tohu* is marked by ego, non-interconnectivity and non-responsibility. It is a reality in which each *sefira* is on its own, and there is no room for others or for interplay. As a result, there is a meltdown of the world of *tohu*, and eventually there emerges a universe of *tikun*. Until three years of age, children orbit in the world of self-absorbed *tohu*. There is no room for sharing toys or for understanding others. The way they see it, they need to *mispashet*/spread themselves over as many things as possible, and claim everything in sight as their own. If such behavior would continue throughout life, if ego were to never be checked or counterbalanced, there would ultimately be an internal meltdown.

Being of the world of *tohu*, this young child runs about wild, with long uncut hair. The child is hairy as the physical embodiment of *tohu* is the Biblical character of *Esav*, the brother of *Yakov*. Upon him, the *Torah* relates this idea of hair (*Bereishis* 25:25).

Now that the child has reached a ripe age of three, a haircut is due to facilitate movement into the world of *tikun*. We are born wild, yet there is no genuine spirituality without ethics. There needs to be a taming of the wild, a *tikun*.

Getting a haircut and leaving the *peyos* is a symbolic representation of movement into *tikun*. A limit is set to the child's *hispashtus*, and he moves into a level of maturity by taking the wild, untamed, undisciplined, chaotic reality of babyhood and cutting off the long hair, setting a border. *Peyos*, as previously mentioned, set a boundary, give a limitation to how much of the person extends outwards. At this point, the child has enough understanding and awareness of others, that he can be educated and introduced to a proper framework to exist in a more delineated, descriptive *tikun* existence; a world of order, *egolessness* and sharing.

The border, symbolic of the *peyos*, allows for greater integration, as the child feels secure in who he is, he can appreciate who the other is as well. In Hebrew, a haircut is called *tisporet* from the root word *safar,* which also means boundary. This word is related to the word *sapir*, sapphire in English. From the boundary of the haircut, and *peyos*, a new illumination arises, and the child shines brightly like a sparkling sapphire.

Peyos are generally formed in the shape of a line. The line of *peyos* symbolizes boundary and order. In addition to leaving *peyos*, from the *upsherin* onward, the young boy is trained to wear *tzitzis*. Also called *talis katan*/small *talis*, it is a square garment with *dalet kanfos*/four corners, with eight strings hanging upon each corner. The garment itself is a square, another allusion to a line, a boundary. Yet there are a total of thirty-two strings that dangle from the corners, eight on each corner, symbolizing a penetration of the sharp edged corners and a downward flowing of energy. In its root, the word *tzitzis* is connected with the word *nitzutz*/spark. As with *tzitzis*, sparks burst forth from the four corners and pierce through all squareness and the concept of being boxed in.

Besides the prominent imagery of lines and squares, the idea of *tikun* and order, there is also a healthy counter-dose of circle energy, representing retention of *tohu* energy. If line and square represents order, boundary, finite, circle represents transcendence, boundlessness, infinity. A line is defined with a clear beginning and end, not so with a circle, undefined, without beginning or end.

Peyos are lines; *tzitzis* is square, yet it is a corner garment from which energy flows outside of its parameters, albeit in the form of lines. More apropos is the donning of a *yarmulka*/headcovering, known as a *kipa*, on the head of the young child. Up until the boy was three years old, he boy went without a *yarmulka*, in fact, according to many traditions the boy should not put on a *yarmulka*, even temporarily, before the *Upsherin*, and from this day forward the child puts on a *yarmulka*, a cap that covers the head, and as the head is round so too is the *yarmulka*.

There is an overall movement from *tohu* into *tikun*, from circle reality into line reality, from immaturity into maturity. Yet the purpose is always integration, to learn to move into the maturity of *tikun* without ever completely letting go of the passionate energy of *tohu*, to be responsible people without losing the almost simplistic joyful dispassion of childhood. As we mature, we need to learn to channel "the Infinite Light of *tohu* into the vessels of tik*un*".

Uncut Hair vs. No Hair
&
the Balance In Between

Upsherin is the cutting of the hair. To more deeply understand the nature of this rite of passage, it behooves us to explore what hair is. In the *Zohar*, every strand of hair is viewed as harboring entire universes, but what exactly does this mean? What is unique about hair? And what does human hair represent? Before we can delve deeper into the nature of hair, understanding and deciphering the various forms of male hair (such as head, facial and body) and the hair of the female, we ought to first become familiar with the way hair or the lack thereof is discussed in the *Torah*.

In the *Torah* we find that people committed to a life of holiness and service as the tribe of Levi needed to shave their hair completely, to initiate them into service (*Bamidbar* 8:7) and the *Cohanim*/priests among them were not allowed to grow long hair. The High Priest would cut his hair once a week and the other priests would cut their hair once a month (*Tannis* 17b). By contrast, the *nazir* (*Bamidbar* 6: 1-21), one who takes upon him or herself to be a nazirite, "to separate themselves to G-d" to live a life of holiness, must never cut his hair at all. In fact, the hair is part of their holiness. (6:5)

So there is an act of holiness in the context of long, unkempt, uncut hair, and holiness that demands the cutting of all hair.

Why the difference?

Traditionally, the *nazir* is viewed as an ascetic. This is because a *nazir* refrains from drinking wine, and simply allows his or her hair to run wild.

Gleaning through sources, it becomes apparent that most *nazirim* in Temple times were young and single. As a means to fend off their temptations they would tip into the extreme opposite direction and lead a life, most times it was temporarily, detached and removed from society.

The *nazir* accepted upon himself to live a nazirite life style as a kind of spiritual retreat from the chaotic, aggressive competitive nature of adolescence and youth. Struggling with life, or being weighed down by negative temptations they wished to retreat a bit, stand back, detach themselves from the pleasures of life, such as the drinking of wine represents, and also detaching themselves from life's sorrows, such as death, thus not touching or contacting the dead. They simply wanted to be, and observe, without too much participation in the drama of life, for better or worse.

Notwithstanding the positive role that being a *nazir* could play in terms of healthy spiritual development, a *nazir* represents a type of holiness and dedication that is not intended as a way of life. Life in retreat is ultimately ego-based. In fact, the *nazir* after his stint as a *nazir* needs to bring an offering of atonement, as it were, atoning for refraining from drinking wine. For the time being the life of a *nazir* serves a wonderful purpose, a detachment to further a more focused meaningful involvement. Yet, life as a *nazir* is meant as a time bound retreat, to transcend to later emerge. It is a life of *pelah* (*Bamidbar* 6:2), which means detached, separate, and isolated, whereas life is meant to be lived, fully and with total mindful participation.

The polar opposite of the long-haired *nazir* is the priest, who served without long hair. This too is an extreme, with no ritual contamination and no hair. Though this life was the lot of an entire tribe, it also indicates a life detached from ordinary experiences, thus it was only one tribe's lot and not the entire nation's task.

In between the no hair and the long hair is the short hair reality, which is relevant to all people and applicable to all times.

In the *Torah* we find the idea of having a haircut when a person comes in front of a king, as a sign of respect. *Yosef*/Joseph was thrown into prison, and when the ruler of Egypt heard of his amazing dream interpretation the verse says "Then *Pharaoh* sent and called *Yosef*, and they brought him hastily out of the dungeon; and he shaved himself" (*Bereishis* 41:14).

In Talmudic law the idea of having one's hair cut is a sign of respect, whether taking a haircut in the honor of *Shabbos* or the holidays, or any other momentous event. The *Midrash* speaks of *Rosh Hashanah*/The Day of Judgment as a time when we, in great confidence in the eventual outcome of the heavenly ruling, congregate, dressed in their finest attire, clean, and with our hair nicely trimmed.

As long hair or no hair represents a holiness that is detached from the everyday, mundane reality, the balanced trimmed hair reflects the well-adjusted life of holiness, to live within world and yet to be above, to be above and yet enfolded within. In the words of classic Kabbalistic language, life is to be lived in a condition of "*mati ve'lo mati*/touching and not touching" or "reaching and retreating." In fact, the only way to truly and fully be present in life is by remaining a slight measure above it, as the Kotzker Rebbe used to say, "If you wish to know the world, you need to soar above it".

Ultimately we express our full beingness when our lives mimic our Creator, when we are like our Creator, as it were, embodying both immanence and transcendence, being and non-being. On the one hand to be fully 'drawn within' world, not neglecting nor renouncing the beauty of creation or the value of this physical, and yet remaining somewhat above and transcendent of creation's trivialities.

A little boy until his 'ripe' age of three lives for the most part, a careless, selfish, involved life, certainly not entirely interested or even equipped to participate as a fully integrated member of society. With his long flowing hair, his life of 'detachment' and 'non-responsibility' reminds us of the *nazir* who also chooses to live detached and not responsible. Parents tend to shield their very young ones, and often for good reason, from the sorrows of life. In the same way, in joyful times children at this young age are apt to do their own thing and be in their own world.

And then the next stage of maturation begins, and the baby becomes a child. Borders of self-expansion are set, and the child gets his hair trimmed. Mirroring the child's own development, as the child begins to be more aware of others, and assume more responsibility, as the child is weaned from the cocoon of a protective home to a life within a greater society, and school, the child's hair is cut and the *peyos* are left. The cutting the hair indicates a movement from *nazir*-like existence to a reality where the child can now fully and with awareness participate in the conversation of life.

Three Forms of Head Hair (Detached, Masculine, Feminine)

Now that we have a better grasp on the way head hair is presented in the revealed aspects of *Torah*, we can comfortably move into the deeper dimensions of *Torah*, and explore the nature of hair and what it represents.

Hair grows on mammals for protection to keep the body warm. On a literal level—the literal always being an outer reflection of the deeper—hair is threadlike outgrowth from our skin. On a deeper level, hair is rooted in the space beyond the skin, as it were, beneath the surface of the epidermis. The intensity, measure and level of spiritual energy contained within a strand of hair depend on the interior beneath the surface upon which the hair grows.

Overall, though hair is rooted in and nourished by the body, it contains little to no blood cells or nerves, and can thus be cut off with no pain. Each strand of hair is thin and threadlike and is not individually overwhelming. Hair reflects an energy flow that penetrates the below in a way that is measured and can be appreciated and appropriately accessed, as the word *sa'ar*/hair can be read as *shiur*/measurement. As such, flowing hair represents a flow of energy.

Beginning with hair of the head, there are three forms of such hair:

• In the language of the *Kabbalah*, there is the hair of *Atik*/detached, removed, transcendent of all distinctions; part of the *sefira* of *Keser*/crown, deep desire reality; represented by the hair of the nazirite, both male and female.

• There is the hair of *Zeir Anpin* (*Z'a*)/small face, hair of the male, masculine; *Zeir Anpin* is comprised of the six emotional Divine attributes, otherwise known as the emotional *sefiros*: *chesed*/kindness, *gevurah*/restraint, *tiferes*/compassion, *netzach*/perseverance, *hod*/humility and *yesod*/connection.

• There is the hair of *Nukvah*/receiver, immediacy, presence, feminine, hair of the female, feminine.

Essentially these are three types of head hair: one rooted in *Atik*, another in *Zeir Anpin*, the third in *Nukvah*. Yet each one of these levels is considered an entire *partzuf*/structure on its own. There are a total of five *partzufim*, three of them are *Atik*, *Zeir Anpin* and *Nukvah*, the other two are *Arich Anpin*/long enlarged face, the idea of will and *A'v'A*/intelligence (combination of *Aba*/*chochmah* and *Ima*/*binah*). Each *partzuf* contains the entire arrangement of all the *sefiros*, albeit, occasionally in a *zeir*/smaller, contracted version so that each one is a total structure, a full divine persona, as it were.

Think of the *partzuf* as a hologram, wherein each aspect contains the whole. For example, in the universe of emotions there is also intelligence, the intellect guiding and orienting the emotions; conversely, there are also emotions in the world of intelligence, as emotions stir and affect all intellectual understandings.

Surface observation suggests that the actual hair on the head originates in the skull. Metaphysically speaking, all head hair originates from within the skull, as it were. The deeper source of head hair is "*mosras ha'mochin*/residue of brain", better yet, mind energy, a surplus of excess mind.

The energy that flows from *mochin*/mind in each distinct strand of hair is constricted and limited, much like its thin-shaped nature. Hair contains a slim measure of body energy, and thus can be cut or trimmed with no pain. What is more, the life energy of hair is present within the actual *challal*/hollowed space within each strand. Accordingly, the *chayos*/life energy within hair is the least of the body's, even less than the life energy within nails.

Hair transmits and funnels energy, albeit condensed and contracted in its stream. Paralleling the cosmic structure, every strand of head hair, every blade of thin, lined hair represents a flow of *din*/constriction and limitation, a fine condensed flow of light. *Din* is *tzimtzum*/contraction and concealment.

All head hair is rooted in excess mind. Since *mochin* is a total *partzuf* with a full array of all aspects, within the hair of *mochin* there is hair that is connected with *Keser*, hair associated with *Zeir Anpin* and hair related to *Nukvah*. Since hair is normally associated with *din* and *tzimtzum* the idea of trimming and shortening one's hair, both hair of the male *Zeir Anpin* and hair of the female *Nukvah*, becomes a symbolic gesture. On a deeper level, an initiation of the trimming process dims and eliminates all manifestations of *din* and constriction in one's life.

Though it is common for the head hair to be shortened, at least from time to time, the head hair of a *nazir* is to remain intact as long as he or she is a *nazir*. For the entire duration that a person accepts upon him or herself to live as a *nazir*, the hair shall be allowed to grow as long as possible.

A *nazir*, man or woman, is one chooses to live for a period of life detached and separate from the social norm (this is different from the *nazir olam*/one who dedicates his entire life to this lifestyle). This reflects the divine energy flow of *Keser*, the crown, a space of Transcendence, a place beyond the world of duality. And since there is "no left side [separateness/*din*/*kelipa*] in *Atik*" (*Zohar*), everything within *Atik*/*Keser* reality is *kedushah*/holy, enclosed within Divine Unity and plenty, the hair too of the *nazir* is *kadosh*/holy, as in sublime and removed, and should not be tampered with or trimmed and allowed to grow long, as hair is generally a form of din and *tzimtzum*, the *nazir's* hair is complete and absolute *Rachamim*/Divine mercy. At this level of reality there is a radical transformation of the quality of hair, from *Din*/restrictions and confinements to *Rachamim*/mercy and openness, and thus the hair is holy and should not be cut at all.

Though the condition of *tzimtzum* is non-existent in *Keser*, and the hair of the *nazir* is holy, still, the *nazir* does have hair, which suggests some mode of *din* restriction and concealment, as hair by definition is condensation and compression of energy.

Din and *tzimtzum* of the nazirite's hair is not related to the actual hair itself, so to speak, rather in the manner in which transcendent *Keser*, beyond and above Infinite light is funneled and channeled into a finite creation, comprised of time and space.

There are two moods of *Hashem's* Light that create and sustain creation. There is the transcendent Infinite light, the *Or Ha'Sovev Kol Almim*/light that surrounds all worlds, and there is the immanent present light, the *Or Memale Kol Almim*/finite light that fills all creation. The Creator's reality makes itself manifest as both immanent and all-pervasive finite, as beingness form of life and as light that is transcendent, infinite and beyond-being. Clearly, these images of surrounding and filling lights are not to be taken literally, with spatial linear connotations, as they are both strictly relating to the degree of revelation and their observed presence within world.

Keser is the crown that hovers above creation, the infinite transcendent *sovev* light. The *partzufim* of *Zeir Anpin* and *Nukvah* represent a more delineated, finite, invested form of enclothed *memale* light, *Zeir Anpin* as the light itself and *Nukvah* as the actual embodiment of the light, and its presence within the physical.

In the world of *memale*, the *hamshacha*/drawing down progression of energy flow is "*b'derech ilah v'alul*/in the manner of cause and effect". Since all are linked within a finite paradigm, albeit some higher than others, there can be an organic natural flow from highest into lowest, from cause into effect. In turn, the effect becomes the cause of another effect. The movement of energy can follow a linear path.

With regard to *sovev*, however, getting from a point of infinity to a point of finitude, the *ilah v'alul* construct does not work; any quantitative evolution of infinity cannot produce finitude. A qualitative movement is needed, a quantum leap, a *tzimtzum* where the infinite retracts, as it were, and that is the *hamshacha*/drawing down "*b'derech sa'aros*/in a manner of hair", a revelation through the form of a *tzimtzum*, which now gives rise to the process of *ilah v'alul*/cause and effect.

When there is this little *ha'arah*/slim glimmer of these intense transcendent Infinite lights of *Keser* that become revealed in the form of *hamshacha b'derech sa'aros*, a radical shift ensues. Originally being the source, the light of *memale* eventually filters down to become the light that is vested within finite creation.

As *nazirim* are the living embodiment of *Keser*/detached, transcendent, beyond world, beyond *din* and *tzimtzum*, their hair is holy. Still, since *Keser* lights are channeled into finite creation through *sa'aros*, they too have hair, hair representing restriction.

In the next chapter, the head hair and *peyos* of the male will be explored. For now, let us move from the *nazir*, who can be either male or female, to the nature of non-*nazir* female hair. In truth, this topic deserves a book of its own, but to help better understand the idea of *peyos* and *Upsherin*, we will touch upon the subject, albeit quickly.

The non-*nazir* male, regardless of marital status, trims his (*Zeir Anpin's*) hair to lessen the aspect of *din* and *tzimtzum* and, traditionally, covers at least part of his head and hair with a form of headcovering, such as a *kipa*. On a deeper level, the purpose for this is to cover over *din*. The laws and customs with regard to female *Nukvah* hair are much more intricate and complex.

Today, the common practice for a woman before they are married and enter into an intimate relationship with a man is not to cover her hair, in private or in public. Additionally, there is no strict limit to the length of the hair she wears, as long as it is within the boundaries of modesty. Once a woman is married, however, her hair is to be covered, certainly in public.

There are various ways that hair covering is practiced today, ranging from wearing either a scarf or a hat, to covering the hair with a wig, or even putting on a covering above the wig. For technical and also practical purposes, married women tend to cut their hair shorter than before marriage; this is done for convenience, allowing them to feel more comfortable with a headcovering. With regard to a woman shaving off her hair completely after marriage, this has become more obsolete in recent times. Within the Hungarian and Romanian communities, there are those who have the tradition to shave their heads completely. Yet many great teachers of *Kabbalah* and Halacha strongly discourage this practice.

The male hair (*Zeir Anpin*) is best trimmed short to negate *din*/constrictions and, traditionally, should be covered. This is regardless of the male's marital status. However, a married woman's (*Nukvah*) hair need not be cut very short. According to many, it should not be cut off completely, yet it is required to be covered.

Nukvah is the embodiment of the energy of *memale*/finite light, light that is particularized and perfectly, intimately fitted for the vessel of the receiver. As the female reflects the energy and life force of this universe, the light of *memale*, eliminating all hair would cosmically represent a ceasing of all *memale* energy flow into this universe, a breakdown, as it were, in the process of creation.

There is cutting and there is covering; the difference between the two is that something cut is eliminated completely, while something covered is still present, just not observed by others. Hair that is cut off represents a total eradication of *din*, as the hair is no longer attached to its source of nourishment. Where *din* is still present with hair that is covered, but much less severely. The *din* is not available, as it were, for others to receive, and others cannot be negatively affected by these *dinim*.

Traditionally, a non-*nazir* male cuts his hair short and covers it, albeit often only some of the head and hair with a headcovering, as in a *yarmulka/kipa*; the married female does not necessarily cut her hair very short or shave; nonetheless, there is much greater stringency in regards to covering her hair.

For the male *Zeir Anpin*, there is more potential for an intense aggressive form of *din*-either within oneself or as expressed to others. Thus there needs to be a softening on all levels, both to cut and to cover the hair and to do so before and after marriage. The more genteel *Nukvah* is a reflection of the tender Divine *memale* energy enclothed within every minute of creation, and manifests only according to the abilities of the finite receiver. Therefore, the *Nukvah's* hair can flow more freely: before marriage, without a covering, and after marriage, much more strictly under a covering.

The female is the embodiment of *malchus*/the quality of royalty, receptivity, the feminine dimension of the *sefiros*, the Divine indwelling and presence within creation. Since this world is a place of *din*, with barometers and borders, the feminine who embodies the earth's and the world's energy should thus go with uncovered head hair before marriage, and covered afterwards.

Prior to entering into an intimate relationship with another, a woman's heart and sensuality is private, closed-off. Entering into a relationship implies an opening and offering up of self, thus inviting vulnerability. With the ability to feel love and connect intimately with another person comes the possibility of hurt and heartbreak. Once the valve of giving, of offering oneself to another is open, any parasite, as it were, can gain entry and receive sustenance. Being the embodiment of *memale*, a woman can wear her hair proudly for herself and for her husband, her beloved, without a covering. The enjoyment and nourishment her spouse receives from her *dinim* are gentle, appropriate and properly directed to the receiver, but others, those who simply wish to prey on her openness and vulnerability, receive nourishment that is funneled towards *kelipa*/unholy, the shell which obscures the Divine beauty within everything.

Whenever there is a *yenika*/possibility for someone to receive nourishment from her in a positive form, in this case her spouse, there can also be a *yenika l'chitzonim*/spilling over of her energy to unwelcome outside forces. This is true on all levels, spiritually and physically, macrocosmically and microcosmically, when there is an opening of self to others, all can then receive, both those who use this opening for the positive and those who use it for the negative. When there is a proper receiver, opening up and allowing others to enter can be greatly enriching to the person him or herself; and when there is not, it can be horribly devastating.

If a woman who has not yet entered into a relationship

that is physically intimate in sacred marriage, acts in a way that suggests wanting to be left alone, not desiring physically intimacy, there is little to no possibility for any type of *yenika l'chitzonim*. There is a closing off in this case, a shutting down of all *yenika* of sensuality. Once she enters into a physically intimate relationship in marriage, there is then an opening in the flow of this form of energy. Since she has a holy *yenika* to her spouse, there can also be an unholy *yenika* to *kelipa*, being that hair in general, and female hair in particular, can carry tremendous sensual energy. *Kelipa*, which is nothing more than an apparent concealment of *Hashem's* unity, cannot be nurtured or nourished in a place where there is no nourishment from *kedusha*/the holy. If, however, there is any opening for *kedusha*, there can also be an opening for *kelipa*.

To simplify, the reason there is a difference between head hair that is called *kodesh*/holy with no *din*, as in the *nazir's* hair, verses head hair that has *din* and thus needs to be cut and covered, as in the non-*nazir* male's hair, and hair that is longer and yet more strictly covered, as in a female's hair, is determined by the spiritual root of the hair. When hair is rooted in *Atik*/detached transcendent space, as in the hair of the *nazir*, who him or herself lives a detached existence, than there is no *kelipa* or *din*. Conversely, when hair is rooted in the male *partzuf* of *Zeir Anpin* or the female *partzuf* of *Nukvah*, there is potential for *kelipa*.

Male Hair
&
the Act of Transforming Judgment into Compassion

There are three types of adult male facial hair:

- Head hair
- The beard
- *Peyos*/sidelocks

These three types of male hair have different spiritual symbolism and qualities. There is hair that should be cut and covered, head hair; there is hair that should be allowed to grow, at least to certain lengths and does not need to be covered, the *peyos*; and there is hair that is not allowed to be cut, and certainly not with a razor, the beard.

Being that this work is dedicated to the *Upsherin* of a young boy, only the former two will be explored deeply, the facial hair will only be touched upon.

Head Hair:

Male head hair is associated with *Zeir Anpin*/small face; therefore, it needs to be cut and covered so not to retain an excess of *din.* The act of cutting suggests a rectification, a *tikun* to the aggressive male quality, which is especially important to those male souls who are rooted in the root soul of Kayin/Cain.

When hair is removed, it is done with a razor, which is called a *ta'ar* in the *Torah.* The word *ta'ar* is spelled *Taf, Ayin Reish.* The letter *Taf* is 400, *Ayin* is 70 and *Reish* is 200; in total, the sum is 670, with the *kollel*/the word itself equaling 671. 671 is the same as the name *Ado-noi*/Lord, Master.

The name *Ado-noi* is comprised of 4 Hebrew Letters, *Aleph, Dalet, Nun* and *Yud.* When each of these four letters is spelled out, the total number is 671:

Aleph is comprised of three letters: *Aleph*/1, *Lamed*/30, *Pei*/80 = 111.

Dalet is comprised of three letters: *Dalet*/4, *Lamed*/30, *Taf*/400 = 434.

Nun is comprised of three letters: *Nun*/50, *Vav*/6, *Nun*/50 = 106.

Yud, is comprised of three letters: *Yud*/10, *Vav*/6, *Dalet*/4 = 20.

Adding the totals together, 111 + 434 + 106 + 20 = 671.

Hair on the male head represents *din*, when a person takes a *ta'ar*/ razor, which reflects the Divine quality of *Ado-noi* and cuts his hair, he then sweetens and transforms the *din* of hair into a source of mercy, compassion and blessings.

Ado-noi is a Divine name connected with *Hashem's* attribute, as it were, of indwelling within creation. The name *Ado-noi* is comprised of two words, *Aleph* and *Din*; so *Ado-noi* is *Aleph Din*/ the One in *Din*. In the Name *Ado-noi*, there is the element of *din*/constriction and separation, and yet the *Aleph*, which is one and represents The One, is also present. Therein, there is an *Aleph* within *din*.

Through the act of the *ta'ar*, the name *Ado-noi* transforms *din* into mercy. *Ado-noi* in general is a transformer, as it takes the name of *Hashem*, the Tetragrammaton, which is ineffable, and renders it into a name we can say; otherwise, we are not allowed, nor do we know how to pronounce this name. The name *Hashem* is pronounced as *Ado-noi*.

THE BEARD:

With regards to the hair of the beard, the *Torah* tells us that we are not to eliminate these hairs. The sages of the *Talmud* tell us this means it is not permissible to cut the hair with a *ta'ar*/razor.

The word for facial hair in the *Torah* is *Zakan*. *Zakan* in numeric value is 157. The word *Zakan* is spelled with three Hebrew letters: *Zayin*/7, *Kuf*/100, *Nun*/50 = 157. As there are two sides to the face, 157 twice = 314. 314 is also the numeric value as the Divine name *Sha-dai*. The same *Sha-dai* is spelled three Hebrew letters: *Shin*/300, *Dalet*/4, *Yud*/10 = 314.

Sha'dai means enough. The *Midrash* tells us that as the

world was being created and endlessly expanding, *Hashem* said to the world, "*Shad-dai*/Enough". Enough can also mean perfect. The facial hair is also perfect, with no *din*.

Paradoxically, the word *Shad-dai* denotes both an aspect of destroying, from the word *shoded*/to break and destroy, and an aspect of nurturing, from the word *shadayim*/that which nourishes and nurtures a young suckling. *Sha-dai* is the Divine aspect that nurtures and gives life to creation. The name *Sha-dai* reflects itself in the ebb and flow of creation. Nature is continually creating and self-destroying, building and pulling down in one continuous rhythmic motion. There is constant movement fluctuating back and forth, but in all movements, there is the guiding Divine nurturer protecting and allowing for further growth.

Beard hair represents this natural flow of creation and thus should to be left alone to flow naturally. Being a reflection of the natural flow of creation, the beard also comes to represent the Thirteen Attributes of Mercy, enumerated in the book of *Shemos*/Exodus (34:6-7), as in "Hashem, Hashem, (which are not counted as part of the thirteen according to many opinions), *E-l*/G-d, Merciful and gracious, slow to anger, abundant in loving-kindness and truth, remembering kindness..." and in the book of *Michah* (7:18-20). These thirteen qualities are the attributes through which Hashem governs the world.

In their higher form of revelation, the Thirteen Attributes are rooted in *Keser*/crown, a space where there is no *din*, concealment or constriction, and so it, too, is holy as the hair of the *nazir* and should not be eliminated. There is no reason to put the *ta'ar,* instrument of transformation, to the beard as the facial hair embodies the quality of the Thirteen Attributes of Mercy, Pure compassion and an Infinite Source for blessings, both spiritually and physically.

It should be noted that while females do not, as a rule, have facial beard hair, they still embody, in the place where male hair grows, the structure of these Thirteen Attributes of Mercy.

Peyos:

With regards to a boy having an *upsherin,* the head hair and the *peyos* are the most important, as his head hair is cut shorter and his *peyos* are left.

Peah, as explained earlier, is the quality of *Elokim* (both *peah,* singular for *peyos,* and *Elokim* are 86 in numeric value), setting a border and a boundary. Yet *peyos* are rooted in a very high spiritual place, even beyond the facial hair of the beard. The facial hair is a reflection of the Thirteen Attributes of Mercy, which begins with *E-l,* however, both *peah,* one on each side, is rooted in the two names of *Hashem,* as in "*Hashem, Hashem*" that proceed *E-l.* The Thirteen Attributes begins with the word "*Hashem, Hashem, E-l*", yet the actual first attribute is *E-l.* Literally, where the *peyos* end, the facial hair of the Thirteen Attributes begins.

The hair of the *peyos* embodies both the quality of

Hashem and *Elokim*, and the unity between them, how the Infinite Transcendence of *Hashem* becomes manifest within the finite, immediate dimensions of *Elokim*, the place of *din*, time and space. The possibility for this unity of seeming opposites is because the *peyos* are rooted in "*Hashem, Hashem,*" the Infinite; and on a deeper level, the Infinite and the finite are one.

Peyos are connected with the name *Hashem,* with how the name is revealed in *chiluf*/exchange. The name of *Yud-Hei-Vav-Hei*, in the exchange of *At-Bash* (where the first letter of the *Aleph Beis* becomes interchangeable with the last letter, and the second letter with the second to the last, and the third with the third to the last, and so forth) is *Mem* (for *Yud*), *Tzadik* (for *Hei*), *Pei* (for *Vav*) and Tzadik (for Hei). In numeric value, the name *Mem*/40 *Tzadik*/90 *Pei*/80, *Tzadik*/90 = 300.

300 is also the name *Elokim* in full numeric value. *Elokim* on its own is 86, as *peah*, yet when the letters of *Elokim* are filled, they equal 300. *Elokim* is comprised of five Hebrew letters:

Aleph/1, *Lamed*/30, Hei/5, *Yud*/10, *Mem*/40.

Aleph in full is *Aleph*/1, *Lamed*/30, *Pei*/80=111.

Lamed in full is *Lamed*/30, *Mem*/40, *Dalet*/4 = 74.

Hei in full is Hei/5, *Yud* /10 = 15.

Yud in full is *Yud*/10, *Vav*/ 6, *Dalet*/4 = 20.

Mem in full is *Mem*/40, final *Mem*/40 = 80.

111+ 74 + 15+ 20+ 80 = 300

Peyos are both *Elokim*/constriction and *Hashem*/Infinity, and the unity between them, the Infinite being infused within the finite. So while we generally need to use a *ta'ar*, which embodies the quality of *Ado-noi*, a transformative tool, and cut the head hair of the male, the *peyos* need to be left, leaving some space for *din*. The *peyos* are much like a bridge between Infinity and the finite. Literally positioned between the head hair and the (eventual) facial hair, the *peyos* serve as both a partition separating the negative hair from the positive hair, the hair of pure *din* from the hair of the Thirteen Attributes of Mercy, as well as bridging the highest spiritual space into the lowest physical space.

Now we can better understand why the *Upsherin* occurs at the age of three. Besides the fact that the age of three is a transitional period for a child, especially for a boy, on a deeper level, this is because up until three, or there about, a child does not have the power to transform *din* into *rachamim*. Transformation demands awareness, a heightened, evolved consciousness of how to separate from certain ideas and how to integrate others. A young child lacks this discerning and *havdalah*/separating quality.

The fact that a young toddler functions from a place with less *havdalah* is connected with his inability to practice or perceive *havdalah*, whether from his mother, or he generally does not yet have a sense of order where everything and everyone belongs; so he wears his hair long. Upon transitioning from a toddler into a boy, which shows up as him being weaned from his mother, there is now a stricter sense of order, and the child begins to understand *havdalah* better. He begins to understand his place and his parents' place.

Upsherin has almost become synonymous with *Lag B'Omer*/the thirty-third day of the *Omer*. This is because during the period of the *Omer*, from *Pesach*/Passover until a few days before *Shavuos,* is a time of national mourning for the death of the 24,000 students of Rabbi Akiva and the cutting of hair is forbidden, except on the day of *Lag B'Omer*. So any boy who turns three in that period can only cut his hair on that day. Also, the affinity between the two is related to the fact that one of the earliest sources of this custom is found in the writings of the Arizal, who took his young son on *Lag B'Omer* to Miron and gave him a haircut. On a deeper level, the haircutting and the day of *Lag B'Omer* are intricately connected.

The forty-nine days between *Pesach* and *Shavuos* represent forty-nine steps of personal development, going from the freedom experiences on *Pesach* to the assuming of responsibility of *Shavuos*, when we receive the *Torah*. There are the seven primary emotional *sefiros*/attributes and each of these attributes on its own without a healthy dose mixed in from the others creates a condition of *tohu*/confusion, chaos. To establish a *tikun*/correction and order, there needs to be a blending of the attributes so that each one of the seven contains all of the other, thus the sum total is forty-nine. *Lag B'Omer* is the day we celebrate both the passing of Rabbi Shimon Bar Yochai (one of the remaining students of Rabbi Akiva) and the day the students of Rabbi Akiva either ceased dying, or did not die on that day. The thirty-third day, which in terms of the *sefiros* is either *Hod* of *Hod*/glory of glory, counting from the down up (from one to forty nine) or *Tifferes* of *Tifferes*/ beauty of beauty, counting from the up down (from forty nine to one). *Lag B'Omer* embodies the quality of perfect *tikun*; as such, it is a most auspicious time to cut a young boy's hair.

Once a child is three and begins to leave a paradigm of *tohu* and enters the world of *tikun,* it is now the appropriate time to cut the hair shorter, leave the *peyos*, setting boundaries and borders, and educate the child in the ways of order and discipline. Of course, with measured discipline we must also insure that the child continues to be treated with unconditional love and given plenty of room for self-expression.

Customs of the Upsherin & the Order of the Ceremony

The child is dressed in special clothes, wearing a Kipa and Tzitzis.

A blessing should be made for the Tzitzis (if not yet said in the morning, when the Tzitzis were first put on.) Standing up, and wearing the Tzitzis the child should hold the Tzitzis (that is, the strings of all four corners) in his right hand (if left- handed, in his left hand) and recite:

ברוך אתה ה' א-לוהינו מלך העולם,
אשר קדשנו במצותיו וצונו על מצות ציצת.

Transliteration: Barukh atah Ado-nai Elohei-nu melekh ha-olam, asher kid'shanu b'mitzvosav, v'tzivanu al mitzvas tzitzis.

Translation: Blessed are You, Ado-noi, our G-d, King of the universe, who has sanctified us with His commandments, and commanded us concerning the Mitzvah of Tzitzis.

After the blessing the child should kiss the Tzitzis.

Begin the Upsherin ceremony by offering a blessing to

the child. The blessing should be offered by the parents, grandparents, or a respected rabbinic figure.

Many have the custom for a *Cohen*/member of the priestly tribe to recite the priestly blessings:

יְבָרֶכְךָ ה׳ וְיִשְׁמְרֶךָ

יָאֵר ה׳ פָּנָיו אֵלֶיךָ, וִיחֻנֶּךָּ

יִשָּׂא ה׳ פָּנָיו אֵלֶיךָ, וְיָשֵׂם לְךָ שָׁלוֹם

Translation:

May Hashem bless you and guard you
May Hashem make His face shine on you
and show favor to you
May Hashem lift up His face on you
and give you peace

The initial cutting of the hair is done ceremonially, and in a festive mood.

There are those who customarily begin to snip the hair from the place where the *peyos* grow, on the side of the head, to indicate that the purpose of the hair cut is to leave the *peyos*. There are others who begin the snipping from above the forehead, the place where the *tefilin* will eventually be worn. Yet there are still others who begin snipping from the middle of the head, where the hair is most dense.

There is a custom for a *Cohen*/member of the priestly

tribe to take the first cut; others reserve this privilege for an elderly rabbinic figure.

Many begin with the father taking the first snip, as he is primarily responsible for the boy's education and is thus liable to leave the *peyos*. Afterwards, many continue with the mother, as the mother is traditionally the primary nurturer of a young child's development.

Other members of the family, if they wish, can also take part in the cutting, as well as friends of the family.

When cutting the hair there are those that have the custom to recite the words of the verse:

לֹא תַקִּפוּ פְּאַת רֹאשְׁכֶם

Translation: You shall not round the corners of your heads. (Vayikra 19:27)

When taking a cut of hair offer the child a dollar or some change, to train the child in the *mitzvah* of *tzedakah*. The child takes the money and deposits it into a *pushka*/ charity box that is next to him, so the child is giving Tzedakah at the ceremony.

The money for charity is in addition to giving the child money or a gift upon this momentous occasion. The gifts leave the child with a positive feeling of his initiation into *mitzvas*.

While most people do the below at a later point in time, when they bring the boy for the first time to *cheider*/school, there is also a custom to take a sheet which the *Aleph Beis* written on it and cover the sheet with honey and have the child lick the honey. In this way, the *Torah* shall be to him "sweet upon his tongue".

The *Talmud* (*Sukka* 42a) teaches that from the moment a child learns to speak, his father should teach him:

תּוֹרָה צִוָּה לָנוּ, מֹשֶׁה מוֹרָשָׁה, קְהִלַּת יַעֲקֹב

Translation: The *Torah* was transmitted to us through *Moshe*, an inheritance for all the Jewish people (*Devarim* 33:4).

These are the first words he should be taught to say. Many have the custom to recite this verse with the child at the celebration, as well as the verse of *Shema*;

שְׁמַע, יִשְׂרָאֵל ה׳ א-לוהינו ה׳ אֶחָד

Translation: Hear *Israel*, *Hashem* is our G-d, *Hashem* is One (*Devarim* 6:4).

After the hair is cut, there is a custom to hide or bury it.

A charming custom is to take the boy's hair, weigh it and then give the equivalent of value in gold or silver, or to exchange it for money, and then give that money to charity. Many give to a charity that is related to the eventual education of this young boy, such as to a *yeshivah*.

During the ceremony, it is appropriate for someone to teach *Torah*.

The ceremony is primarily an act of initiating the child into *Torah* and *mitzvas*, beginning with the child wearing a *kipa*/head-covering and the garment of *tztizis*.

Afterword

Having explored the deeper symbolism of hair and the purpose of the leaving of the *peyos*, it is our hope and prayer that very speedily we merit a time when "a star will arise from *Yakov*...and burst through the *peyos* of the Moabite nation" (*Bamidbar* 24:17). Beyond the literal interpretation of this verse, this can also refer to the breaking of all boundaries and restrictions.

Today, we need the element of *din*, albeit in a small measure, to insure the Divine flow of energy into our world. During our internal and external, personal and collective exile, we need a measure of constriction. Yet there will come a time when perception will be transparent, and a "star will arise...and burst through all limitations"

May we merit to observe the fulfillment of this prophecy speedily in our days, with the coming of *Moshiach*. *Amen*, May it be Hashem's will.

SELECTED SOURCES

In Hebrew the haircut is called *Tisporet*. Many Arabic speaking Jews call this celebration *Chalkah* – from the Arabic word Lakya for haircut. Note *Bereishis*. 27:12 where the word Chalak refers to a lock of hair.

The Ari went to the gravesite of Rabbi Shimon Bar Yachai with his child Moshe to give him a hair cut on the thirty third day of the *Omer*. *Shar Ha'Kavanos* Inyan Pesach. Derush 12. This is clearly an older custom, as R Chaim writes "*minhag yaduah* –a known custom. Note: Teshuvas *Radbaz*. 2: Siman 608. According to strict *Halachah*/law a child, even today, can have a haircut on the day his born, certainly if the hair is getting in his way. R. Chaim Kanevsky. *Sha'alas Rav.* , 1: 15. p. 72. Yet, the *Minhag*/custom is to wait, certainly according to Kabbalah.

Being that the hair cutting ceremony is a joyful occasion, many have the custom to play music at the celebration. *Sdei Chemed*. Asifas Dinim. Maareches Beis Ha'Kneses. Os 10.

Early sources write that the first cutting is allowed from when the child is 13 weeks. Others speak of when the child is nine months. Or when the child is 2 years. Or even at 4 years. *Leket Yosher*. Hiechal Avodas Hashem. 2.p. 179. *Teshuvas Peulas Tzadik*. 3. Siman 236. (Note *Rashi Berieshis* 21:8.) *Keser Shem Tov*. (Gagin) 1-2. p. 591. *Igros Kodesh*. Vol. 11.p. 60. In Talmudic times, and apparently in times prior there was no custom as to when to cut the hair, in fact occasionally the baby's hair was cut when he was yet a small infant. See Talmud *Moed Katan* 14a.

Three was the age Avraham recognized his Creator. *Nedarin*. 32a. *Midrash Tanchumah*. Parshas Vayeira. 22.

The letter Gimel in the word VaHisgalach–and he shall shave (*Vayikra* 13:33.) is large. Perhaps hinting to the cutting of the hair at the age of three, as the letter Gimel is the number equivalent of three. Also, when it says with regards to Yitzchak, that Avraham "made a great feast the same day that Yitzchak was weaned." *Berieshis* 21:8. The word the Torah uses for weaned is *Va'yigamel* which phonetically is related to the word *Gimel*, the third letter in the Aleph Beis, which represents the number three. Though the Pasuk is speaking about a celebration on Yitzchak's second birthday, after twenty four months. *Rashi* ad loc. See also *Shemuel* 1. 1:24.

Orlah is not allowed for the first three years. Kabbalisticaly this has to do with impure spirits that are attached to the trees for the first three years. The first three years is 'the three impure *kelipos*.' *Zohar* 2. p. 244b. *Sharei Orah*. Shar 5. *Pardas Rimonim*. Shar 24. *Likutei Torah*. Kedoshim 29c.

The parallel between Orlah and hair cutting is a relatively new insight, though there are traces for this comparison in the Talmud. *Yerushalmi Peah*. Chap 1: 4. See also: *Tanchuma*, Kedoshim 14. *Chidushie Ha'Ritva* Shavuos in the beginning. See: *Shu't Arugas Ha'bosem*. (Hungarian) Orach Chaim. Siman 210.

The Midrash speaks about four forms of Orlah. *Midrash Rabbah*. Bereishis 46:5. Orlah of the "ears" *Yirmiyahu* 6:10. Orlah of the mouth. *Shemos* 6:30. Orlah of the heart. *Yirmiyahu*. 9:25. (See: also *Devarim*. 10:16.) And the Orlah of the body. *Bereishis*. 17:11.

For a parallel between Peyos and Peah. See: *Or HaTorah* (Tzemach Tzedek) Vayikra (Hosafos) p. 322.

The main purpose of the first *Upsherin* is the leaving the Peyos. *Sharei Teshuvah* Ohr Ha'chayim Siman 531:7. Also for the purpose is to educate the child. Also, his first cut is like

Reishis Ha'gez –first cutting. The Lubavitcher Rebbe. *Likutei Sichos* Vol. 7 p. 351.

Until the age of the first haircut, there are some who in fact dress the boy in more girl like clothes. This was the custom of the Jews of Yemen. *Yehudi Teiman*. p. 147.

"U'bar Yerech Imo—the fetus is as one of the limbs of the mother", according to R. Eliezer. *Chulin*. 58a. Interestingly, R. Yoseph Engel brings down that a man is called a *father* at the moment of conception, whereas the women is not considered a "mother" until she gives birth. She becomes a mother at birth, until then the child is still part of herself. *Beis Ha'Otzer* Erech Av.

"Isha K'man De'mahila Dami—a women is like circumcised." *Avodah Zarah*. 27a. Perhaps, with regards to girls the more dramatic transitional age is a bit later in life, much more pronounced at the time of maturity, the time of the Bas Mitzvah (12 years), in addition, the transition from a pre-gender to gender is not as drastic for the young girls, as the mother, traditionally is the prime caretaker.

Tzitzis is similar to hair, and breaks the negative Kelipa identified with hair. See eg: *Likutei Halachos*. (R. Nasan of Bereslov) Hilchos Tzitzis. Halacha 4.

The Zohar views every strand of hair as harboring entire universes. *Zohar* Parshas Naso Idra Rabah 129a. Every strand of hair is a distinct conduit of energy, shaped as the letter Vav, the letter that connects. R. Chaim Vital. *Shar Ha'Mitzvas*. Parshas Kedoshim. The Talmud speaks of each hair originated from its own follicle. Hashem says "I have created many hairs in a man's head and for every hair I have created a separate follicle" *Niddah* 52b.

The Zohar elaborates on the various different colors of hair, the lengths, density and so forth and connects them with the various personalities of people. *Tikkunei Zohar*. Tikkun 70.

The Levites cut off their hair completely when they were initiated into service. *Bamidbar* 8:7. The Priests were not allowed to serve with long hair. See Talmud *Taanis* 17b. Yet, as the Zohar notes "The holiness of the Cohen is connected with their hair." *Zohar*. 3. Parshas Naso. p. 127a.

A king needs to cut his hair every day, whereas the high priest once a week. *Ibid.* The Talmud speaks of a particular haircut the high priest, Cohen Gadol, would take. *Sanhedrin* 22b. There were Talmudic sages that would take the same style haircut. *Shabbas* 9b.

The Nazir's hair is holy. See Talmud *Pesachim* 23a. And when cut their hair should be burnt or in other situations buried. Talmud *Temurah* 34a.

There are three prohibitions upon the *nazir:* not to drink wine, not to impure him or her self, and not to cut the hair. Whether the *nazir* is one that does these three, and the 'doing' creates the holiness, or, conversely, a Nazir is one the accepts upon himself to be more 'holy' and as a result does not violate these three prohibitions, is debated.

Additionally, the question is whether these three have the same implications. Is the holiness the not drinking wine, and thus, the result not to cut the hair, or, is the *nazir* one who does not drink wine and grow his hair. The Rambam asserts that the Mitzvah of a *nazir* is to accept upon himself to grow his hair and not to drink wine. (*Safer Hamitzvos* Mitzvah 92) while the *Chinuch* writes (Mitzvah 374) the *nazir* is one who refrains from drinking wine, and thus the Mitzvah is that he should grow his hair. According to the Rambam, the actual idea of *nazir* is to not shave and not drink wine. While the Chinuch holds, that the holiness of the *nazir* is that he chooses not to drink wine, and as a result such a person does not shave his or her hair. *Avnei Meluim* Siman 15, and Siman 22.

Traditionally an excess of wine is seen to lead to sin, thus "One who sees a wayward wife in her state of degradation should prohibit himself from wine." *Sotah.* 2a.

Most *nezirim* were single. With regards to the *nazir* the verse says, "to his father or mother, brother or sister he should not defile himself" (*Bamidbar* 6:7) Why not mention his *children* as it says with regards to a Cohen? (*Vayikra.* 21:2) That is because most of them did not have yet children, as they were single. R. Yakkov Kamenetzki. *Emes L'Yakkov.* Nosa. p. 223. Josephus writes of the custom among single men to become *nezirim*. *Josephus,* Against Apian Book 2. Chap 25. Note: *Amus* Chap 2: 11.

Nazir as a sinner, for refraining from wine. *Tannis* 11a. Note: Yerushalmi end of *Kedushin*.

Yoseph trimmed hair in honor of the king. *Bereishis* 41:14. See also: Talmud *Megilah* 16a.

In honor of Shabbas one should take a haircut. See *Tannis* 29b. *Yevamos* 43a. Also in honor of Yom Tov. See *Moed Katan* 13a. With regards to Rosh Hashanah, see: *Tur* Orach Chaim. Siman. 581. *Midrash Rabbah* VaYikra. Parsha 29. See also: R. Yitzchak Abuhav. *Menoras HaMaor.* Ner 5. Klal 2. Part 1. Chap. 1: 5. p 291 regarding the beard.

The sages tell us that a king should cut his hair each day. Why should a king to cut his hair every day? R. Abba Ben Zavda said, this is because, as the Torah says, "Your eyes shall see the king in his beauty." *Tannis* 17a. So in general a cut head of hair is considered for a man more beautiful. Yet, see

Rambam Madah. *Hilchos De'as*. Chap 4. Halacha 19. *Kli Yakar*. Bereishis. 25:25.

Hair of *Atik*, *zeir anpin*, and *nukvah*. See: Arizal. *Ta'amei Hamitzvos* Parshas Kedoshim. Certain hair is holy and certain hair can be the source for a Yenikah L'Chitzonim. *Derech Mitzvosecha*. Mitzvas Tigalachas Metzorah. See also: *Or Ha'Torah*. Parshas Emor. pp. 588-93.

Nazirs hair is the source of *memalah*, the light of *sovev*. *Likutei Torah* Parshas Emor. 32a.

There are two aspects to the covering of the male head; one is the issue of "respect" sensing the One above, the other is related to covering of Din. Already in Talmudic times the custom was for men to cover their heads, as the Gemara says: "Rav Hunah the son of Rav Yehoshua would not walk four cubits bareheaded, saying: The Shechinah is above my head." *Kedushim* 31a. See also *Shabbas* 118b. Meseches *Sofrim*. 14: 15. (Though note *Nedarim* 30b. "Men sometimes cover their heads and sometimes do not, women's hair is always covered, and children also go bareheaded.") From the above sources it appears that the wearing of a headcovering is merely an act of Chassidus–piety. Yet the Beis Yoseph understands the wearing of a headcovering outside as an obligation (certainly today),and not merely an act of extra measure of piety. See *Perisha*. Orach Chaim. 2:6. See also *Taz* with regards to today. *Taz*. Orach Chaim. 8:3. Note: *Zohar*. Parshas Balak.

There are also two aspects to women covering her hair; one is the issue of Tznius–modesty, inwardness, either because of Da'as Moshe or Da'as Yehuudis, and the other the issue of Din and the Yenika/drawing forth to "outside forces", though with women these two issues are related. The idea of inwardness and modesty is not to be viewed as an expression of submission or shame, rather as a symbol of resistance to the commodification of the body, an act of liberation. The Mechaber rules that women "both married and unmarried (ie; once married, *Chelkak Mechokek, Beis Shmuel, Dagul Me'revavah*, ad loc) should not go out in the marketplace with their heads uncovered." *Even Ezra*. Siman 21:2. The *Levush* quotes the words of the Mechaber and adds "and there is a deeper meaning according to Kabbalah." The entire conversation in this work on Upsherin is with regards to covering male and female hair strictly from the point of view of hair as Din, not dealing with the issue of Tznius. Clearly the other issue for males need to also be taken into consideration, as for example, a hairless male should still wear a Kipa.

With the female the idea of Tznius and Din are more interrelated. Thus in a world of perfection and Unity, if there was absolutely no Yenikah to *outside forces* than perhaps there would also be no issue with hair and Tznius, as it says with regards to Adam and Chava/Eve in the Garden of Eden; "And they were both naked...and were not ashamed." (*Bereishis*. 2:25) (Note also with regards to the Cohen viewing the uncovered hair. *Bamidbar* 5:18. *Sotah*. 8a) We find regarding Olam Habah –the perfect world to come that the prophet predicts; "Then... and from the streets of Jerusalem the voice of joy and the voice of gladness, the voice of the bridegroom and the voice of the *bride*." (*Yirmiyahu* 7:34) Or as *Zecharyah* says; "Old men and old women will yet sit in the streets of Jerusalem" (8:4.) Though, generally Koll Isha is Erva as hair, *Berachos* 24a, and there is still a need for separation in the earlier stages of Moshiach, *Sukkah* 52b, yet these prophecies are talking about Olam Habah (*Tosefos*. *Makkos* 24b), which is the most perfect, integrated, unified state possible.

Hair comes from *Mosras Ha'Mochin*—residue of brain, and their *Hamshacha*/ drawing down is not by the way of "cause and effect." R. DovBer of Chabad. *Imrei Binah* 2. p. 22c.

With regards to shaving the head completely, it appears that in Medieval European Jewry it was the common custom, until it was forbidden by a decree of the Czar in 1851. The custom remained in places in Eastern Europe which were not under Russian rule, such as Hungary and Romania. Yet, in the Torah shaving off all the hair for a woman was viewed as rendering the women less attractive. *Devarim* 21: 10-14. Rashi ad loc. In fact, the Gemarah speaks of the Creator grooming Chava's/Eve's hair and then presenting her to Adam. *Berachos* 61a. *Eruvin* 18a. *Nidah* 45b. The Arizal teaches that a woman should not cut her head hair completely. *Shar Hamitzvos* Parshas Kedoshim. *Shulchan Aruch Arizal.* Siman 181:1. Similarly, the Lubavitcher Rebbe strongly discourages the shaving of the head completely. *Sha'arei Halacho U'Minhag.* Vol. 4. p. 141. (Note regarding long hair. *Eruvin* 100b. Note: *Pesachim* 110a.) With regards to Nukvah and hair on the other parts of the Nukavah's body see: *Sanhedrin* 21a. Rashi. Note also *Pesachim* 43a. When Keneses Yisrael (whom Nukvah is an embodiment) is in an elevated state then there is no Kelipa (hair) surrounding the body. Rabbi Yoseph Caro. *Magid Mesharim.* Parshas VaYigash. The Zohar speaks of the cutting the hair of the body of Nukvah before the Yichud with Duchrah. *Zohar* 3. p. 79a. Parshas Emor. *Zohar* 3. Parshas Naso. p. 127a.

Shaving the head completely is seen in the Torah as an act *Nivul*/distastefulness. *Devarim.* 21:12. *Rashi.* However, the *Ramban*, ad loc, views the act of cutting off the hair as an act of mourning. See also: Rambam. *Morah Nevuchim.* 3:41. The prophet Yirmiyahu says: "Cut off your hair, O Jerusalem, and throw it away, and take up a lamentation on the high hills...(7:29) Interestingly, the Halacha is that a mourner is not allowed to cut his hair. *Meod Katan.* 14b. Shaving all the hair was also done in certain situations as an act towards purification. *Vayikra* 14:9.

Hair carries sensual energy, and thus can become a source

for Yenika to inappropriate Kelipa vessels. (This Yenika is available to Kelipa when there is a Yenika for Kedusha/her spouse. When there is no Yenika to Kedusha there can be no Yenika for Kelipa. Hosafos. *Likutei Sichos.* 23. Parshas Nasso. *Likutei Torah.* Vayikra. 24a. 32a.) Though normally this negative potential refers to female hair, *Berachos* 24a, male hair that is worn in a particular fashion can also be a source of Kelipa. *Zohar.* 1. p. 166b. *Tanya. Kuntras Acharon.* 5. See also: *Kedushas Levi.* Parshas Yisro. p. 99. See Talmud *Rosh Hashanah* 26b. Note *Sotah* 9b, with regards to Avshalom.

There is a Torah prohibition against the total elimination of facial hair. *Vayikra.* 19:27. *Makos.* 21:a. *Torah's Kohanim.* Parshas Kedoshim. 6:4. *Kidushin.* 35b. The sages tell us that this means with a Ta'ar/ Razor. *Makos.* 20a.

With regards to the Name Sha-dai see: *Midrash Rabbah* Bereishis. 5: 8.

The "Thirteen Attributes" as related in the Book of Shemos (34:5-7): ("Hashem, Hashem,) "E-l, Merciful and gracious, slow to anger, abundant in loving-kindness and truth, remembering kindness for thousands [of generations], forgiving iniquity and transgression and sin [of those who repent], but not clearing the guilt [of those who do not repent], passing along the sins of the fathers on the children to the third and fourth [generation]." The "Thirteen Attributes" as related in the Book of Michah (7:18-20): "Who is a God like You—Who bears transgression and pardons the wrongdoing of the remnant of His heritage. [He] does not sustain His anger forever, for He desires loving kindness. He will once more have compassion on us [and] forget our transgressions, and [He] will hurl all our sins into the depths of the ocean. [O God] grant truth to Yaakov [and] loving-kindness to Avraham as You vowed to our forefathers long ago."

Thirteen Attributes of Mercy from the book of Shemos are the lower Attributes, whereas the Thirteen Attributes from the book of Michah are the higher. They are rooted in Keser, a space where there is no Din. *Zohar* 3. p. 131a. Certainly, these "attributes" are not meant to be understood as inherent qualities within Hashem, rather as the method of Hashem's activity, by which Hashem governs the world. Rambam. *Moreh Nevuchim.* 1: 52. See also: R. Menachem Rekanti Parshas Va'Yechi. *Shomer Emunim* Part 1.

There is great debate in Halacha whether the prohibition for the male to cut the facial hair is limited to a Ta'ar or a similar tool, but not for example with a scissor, or whether it extends to any form of cutting.

The male beard, Diknah is connected with the "thirteen attributes of mercy." *Zohar* 3. (Parshas Nosa. Idrah Rabbah) 131a. Though this concept seems related only to males, (who have beards) in truth it is also related to females. In general, in Kisvei Arizal/ the writings of the Arizal it says that Malchus has no Diknah. Yet, in *Shar HaKelalim.* p. 41, it is written that Malchus does have Diknah, (not Diknah itself, as women generally do not have facial hair), rather, the place of the Diknah. R. Moshe Chaim Luzzato, the Ramchal, elaborates on how within the Nukvah of Leah there are six Tikunie Diknah and how on the level of Rachel there are four Tikunim. The Ramchal also said that the main purpose his soul came down to this world was to reveal this truth.

The Torah and the sages do not offer a specific measurement of how many hairs need to be left as Peyos. The Rambam writes there should be a least 4 (or 40) hairs. *Rambam.* Hilchos Akum. 12:6. (Kapach) The Shulchan Aruch rules that the entire space on the side is considered Peyos. *Yorah Deah.* Siman 181:9. See also: *Shar HaMitzvas* (Arizal) Parshas Kedoshim. The length of the Peyos is (at least) until the edge of the lobe of the ear. Shulchan Aruch *Ibid.* The Arizal as an adult would cut his Peyos once they reached the hair of the beard. *Shar Hamitzvos* Ibid. Shulchan Aruch Arizal. Siman 181:2. See also: *Beis Lechem Yehudah.* Yorah Deah 181:1. *Darchei Teshuvah.* Ibid. 17.

The two Peyos are rooted in the "Hashem, Hashem" before the Thirteen Attributes of Mercy. R. Tzvi Elimelech of Dinav. *Bnei Yissaschar.* Mamorei Chodesh Elul. 2:2.

The Peyos are the Parsah/ partition between the ten Sefiros as they are within Galgaltah/crown of the head, i.e., hair of the head, and the thirteen attributes of mercy, ie; facial hair. Rashab. *Hemshech Ayin Beis.* Vol. 2. pp 952-961.

Many have the custom to have the Upshernish in a Shul/ synagogue. See *Sdei Chemed.* Asifas Dinim. Maareches Beis Ha'Kneses. Os 10.

Regarding bringing a child into Cheder and covering the Aleph Bet with honey and having the child lick the letters, see *Kav Ha'Yasshar.* Chap 72. p. 245.

With regards to weighing a child's hair and giving to equivalent to charity. Teshuvas *Radbaz.* 2: Siman 608. Note Talmud *Yuma* 38a with regards to a mother weighing the child and giving the equivalent of gold to the Temple. We do find in Tanach that hair was weighed, with regards to Avhshalom. "But in all Israel there was none so much praised as Absalom for his beauty...And when he shaved his head...because the hair was heavy on him...he weighed the hair of his head at two hundred shekels according to the king's weight. *Shmuel* 2. 14: 25-26. See *Ralbag* ad loc.

One the child is three years old we ought to teach them the verses of Torah of "Shema Yisrael..." and "The Torah was transmitted..." Note R. Chaim Ben Atar. *Ohr Hachaim*. Vayikra 19. Note: *Sukka* 42a regarding a father teaching his child the verse of Shema and the verse "The Torah was transmitted..." The simple meaning in reference to Shema is the Mitzvah of reading Shema, that the father should teach his child to say the Shema. Rashi, however, understand that there is no Mitzvah to teach the child how to say the Shema Rashi *Berachos* 20a. Rather the saying of Shema is part of educating the child in the Mitzvah of learning Torah. See also: *Biur Ha'Grah. Shulchan Aruch*. Orach Chaim. Siman 70. See also *Hilchos Talmud Torah*. Admur Ha'Zaken. 1:1. From the time of the *Upsherin* we should educate the child in the wearing Tzitzis, morning blessings, blessings before and after eating, and the saying of the Shema before going to sleep. *Hayom Yom*. Daled Iyyar. With regards to Tzitzis see: *Kitzur Shalah*. Inyanei Tzitzis.

MAPPING THE THIRTEEN ATTRIBUTES OF MERCY

In the book of Shemos/Exodus, after the episode of the Golden Calf, Moshe/Moses re-ascends to the Divine Presence to seek atonement for the people. "If you do not forgive them, wipe me out of this book," he declares. He goes a step further and asks to see Hashem's glory. Hashem says, "You will not see my face... but my back." As Hashem 'passes by', He reveals "The Thirteen Attributes of Mercy." The Talmud envisions Hashem as wearing a tallis, enwrapped in the Attributes.

The Zohar correlate these thirteen with a parallel thirteen found in the Book of Michah. The Arizal correlates the Shemos attributes with the various parts of the Divine "Beard" (reflected in the human beard). The Arizal also correlates these attributes with the Sefiros within Keser. Some sages say that the way to activate the Attributes is simply by reciting them in a group. The RaMaK suggests that they must be actively embodied, and in Tomer Devorah he describes how to do this with regards to the Thirteen Attributes of Michah. He says a person should become like his Master.

Rashi begins counting from the name/attribute Keil. This perhaps implies that Hashem Hashem (usually counted as 1 and 2), here symbolize Divine Essence/Atzmus. The Thirteen are therefore revelations that flow from Keser, Crown, which corresponds to the world of Atzilus, the realmless realm of unmanifest manifestations of Essence.

Keser is above fixed categories of mercy and judgment. This reminds us that each of the Thirteen is inherently paradoxical. When to us it seems that the path of embodiment is unhealthy or merely "co-dependent enabling", we're forgetting that theses are Divine Attributes within Keser. We cannot approach them from a "victimized" or reactive or dualistic consciousness. Embodying them presumes self-mastery. Also, all of these embodiment practices are only real if they are done within the context of Halacha/law. Halachicaly, we must act to prevent a violent person from hurting people, but this is putting Hashem's judgment into effect, not ours. We can remain merciful and positive. Theoretically then, we could actively embody forgiveness toward someone even while we're placing them in prison.

How do you become like your Master—how do embody Keser? Through action. Attributes 1-8 are more revealed. As we rise higher and enter Keser of Keser, we begin to embody more interior attributes of Hashem, so to speak. Thus, 9-13 are similar to 1-8, but are more radically compassionate. The highest levels, the mind/mochin or ChaBaD or ultimate reasoning of Keser is not revealed. It is our mission to reveal the mochin of Keser, and we do this through Torah.

	Attribute as revealed by/to the prophet Michah	Attribute as revealed by/ to Moshe Rabbeinu	Part of the Divine "Beard", reflected in the human beard (Arizal)	Sefirah (Arizal)
1	Mi Keil Kamocha Who is like You, G-d!	Keil G-d	Small hairs under Peyos	Malchus of Chochma of Keser
2	Nosei Avon Who "lifts" iniquity	Rachum Merciful	Moustache (Halachically one can trim or even remove)	Yesod of Chochma of Keser
3	V'oveir al Pesha And overlooks transgression	Chanun Gracious	Hairless part in indentation under nose (also called Ha'Urchah)	Hod of Chochma of Keser
4	Lisheiris Nachalaso For the remembrance of His inheritance	Erech Long/slow	Denser hair under center of lip	Netzach of Chochma of Keser
5	Lo Hechezik Lo'ad Apo Who has not retained His anger eternally	Apayim Anger (Merciful)	Lighter hair under # 4 above	Tiferes of Chochma of Keser

Path of Embodying the Attributes: **a.) Our Master's model 'embodiment'** **b.) Our way of embodiment** **(RaMaK, Tomer Devorah: Thirteen Attributes of the book of Michah)**
a.) The Ultimate Reality is *savlan*/radically tolerant. Even when we rebel, Hashem continues to give us the very life-force we're using against Hashem. b.) We too shall continue to give, even when the recipient is using it against us, like giving a child confidence, even when he uses that confidence for rebellion
a.) Hashem continues this infinite *savlanus* / tolerance to the point that Hashem nourishes the very negativity we ourselves produce, until we finally remove our negativity, or until it 'naturally' lifts. b.) We too shall tolerate others to such measures until they wake up and correct themselves.
a.) Hashem, beyond 'tolerance', lowers Himself to clean up our messes directly. b.) We too shall actively and directly help someone in need, and even someone who hurts us.
a.) Hashem calls us His wife, His daughter, His sister, His mother. He allows us to feel close, or as part of Him. Hashem feels and honors our suffering and joy as His Own, and embraces us accordingly. b.) We too shall feel the suffering and joy of others as our own—the other is us—as all our souls are unified as one. We should seek the best for the other as for ourselves, as we are one.
a.) Hashem can manifest corrective 'anger', but quickly puts aside the manifest attribute of anger, even when we hold onto our anger or are unrepentant. Hashem withholds in hopes that we will return to Him, and seeks to lovingly bring us close. b.) We too shall use loving anger and admonishment when objectively helpful, and when we are emotionally equanimous. We should be ready to drop it instantly. Even when someone is hurting us, we can seek loving reconciliation.

	Attribute as revealed by/to the prophet Michah	Attribute as revealed by/ to Moshe Rabbeinu	Part of the Divine "Beard", reflected in the human beard (Arizal)	Sefirah (Arizal)
6	Ki Chofeitz Chesed Hu For He desires kindness	Rav Chesed Great Kindness	Place where hair starts to widen on cheeks, descending from peyos areas	Gevurah of Chochma of Keser
7	Yashuv V'rachameinu He will again be merciful to us	V'emes And Truth	Hairless place under eyes	Chesed of Chochma of Keser
8	Yichbosh Avonoseinu He will suppress/vanquish our iniquities	Notzer Chesed Preserving Kindness	"Goatee" area under chin: The end, or main part of beard.	Binah of Chochma of Keser
9	V'sachlich bimtzulos yam col chatosam And cast into the depths of the sea all their sins	La'alafim To Thousands	Lighter hairs further under the jaw (more hidden)	Lighter hairs further under the jaw (more hidden)
10	Titein Emes L'yaakov Grant Truth to Jacob	Nosei avon Forgiving (lifting or carrying the burden of) iniquity	Area from base of the neck up to the top of the throat	Netzach of Keser of Keser

Path of Embodying the Attributes: **a.) Our Master's model 'embodiment'** **b.) Our way of embodiment** **(RaMaK, Tomer Devorah: Thirteen Attributes of the book of Michah)**
a.) Hashem desires to see the good, the chesed in us, and He multiplies it in His eyes. He creates angels that overlook our negative deeds, and promote our good deeds. b.) We too shall look to the good in others and 'multiply' it. This is done through gevurah, because we have to overcome our inclination to react to the other's negativity in order to emphasize and look more on the good. Every person has goodness, we need to look for it, maximize their good and minimize their negative.
a.) When we do Teshuvah/return, Hashem loves us even more than before our mistake. Even a tzaddik can't stand where the person of Teshuvah can stand, in Hashem's eyes. b.) When someone wants to return to us and make up, we should allow our intimacy with them to become even greater than before the breakup.
a.) Hashem presses down (yichbosh) our negativity so it doesn't arise into His presence; and what come in front of Hashem, as it were, is only our goodness. b.) We too shall see only goodness in the other, we should suppress and minimize their negativity and thus see more of their goodness.
a.) Though our negative actions have negative effects, in the future Hashem will admonish and take retribution of these "effects" for causing us pain. b.) When we see a destructive person suffering, though suffering because of the effects of their own actions, we shall nonetheless show compassion to them and draw them closer.
a.) Hashem sees that the beinonim, the 'average man' (Yaakov) are acting according to the law, and rewards them measure for measure by being true to them and doing so with compassion. b.) We to shall be true to others, to truly have compassion for others.

	Attribute as revealed by/to the prophet Michah	Attribute as revealed by/ to Moshe Rabbeinu	Part of the Divine "Beard", reflected in the human beard (Arizal)	Sefirah (Arizal)
11	Chesed L'avraham Kindness to Abraham	Vafesha And trans-gression,	Micro-hairs on neck (all equal length)	Tiferes of Keser of Keser
12	Asher Nishbata La'avoseinu As You swore to our ancestors	V'chataah And sin,	The mouth itself	Gevurah of Keser of Keser
13	Mimei Kedem From ancient times	V'nakei And He Cleanses.	Stronger hair under the jaw, closer to neck than #9	Chesed of Keser of Keser

"I remember the affection of your youth...

Path of Embodying the Attributes: **a.) Our Master's model 'embodiment'** **b.) Our way of embodiment** **(RaMaK, Tomer Devorah: Thirteen Attributes of the book of Michah)**
a.) Hashem sees the chasid, one who lovingly goes beyond the letter of the law. Hashem rewards the chasid infinitely, beyond measure for measure. b.) We to shall "surround ourselves with good people"—see everyone around us as worthy of infinite reward, and show compassion to them beyond what is logical.
a.) Hashem rewards people who are lacking any righteousness from the Treasury of Unearned Gifts. He looks back into their ancestry to find merit. b.) Even if we can't find any goodness in someone, we should realize that if they may not be overwhelmingly good their ancestors were holy, and reward them on that basis.
a.) Even when there is no merit to be found in a meritless person's ancestry, then Hashem rewards them on the basis of the kadmonios, the earliest time in that person's life. There was surely some goodness in them when they were an innocent baby. b.) We too shall envision even a completely negative person as he was when nursing from his mother. We can remind this person of this innocent state. This is the ultimate mercy. (Note that the word rachamim/compassion comes from rechem, 'womb')

how you followed Me into the Wilderness..."

—Yirmiyahu, 2:2

Hashem says, "You will not see my face... but my back." As Hashem 'passes by', He reveals "The Thirteen Attributes of Mercy." Shemos 34: 5-7.

The Talmud envisions Hashem wearing a *tallis*. Rosh Hashanah. 17b.

The "Thirteen Attributes" as related in the Book of Shemos (Shemos 34:5-7): *"Hashem, Hashem, Keil, Merciful and gracious, slow to anger, abundant in loving-kindness and truth, remembering kindness for thousands [of generations], forgiving iniquity and transgression and sin [of those who repent], but not clearing the guilt [of those who do not repent], passing along the sins of the fathers on the children to the third and fourth [generation]."*

The "Thirteen Attributes" as related in the Book of Michah (7:18-20): *"Who is a God like You—Who bears transgression and pardons the wrongdoing of the remnant of His heritage. [He] does not sustain His anger forever, for He desires loving kindness. He will once more have compassion on us [and] forget our transgressions, and [He] will hurl all our sins into the depths of the ocean. [O God] grant truth to Yaakov [and] loving-kindness to Avraham as You vowed to our forefathers long ago."*

The Thirteen Attributes of Mercy from Shemos are the lower, while the Thirteen Attributes from the book of Michah are the higher ones. They come from the place where there is no Din. *Zohar* 3. p. 131a. There are the Thirteen Attributes of Arich Anpin/Large Face, and the Nine Attributes in Zair Anpin/Small Face. AriZal. *Shar Ha'kavanas.* Derushie Chazaras Amidah 5. *Eitz Chaim*. Shar 13: 9-11.

These "attributes" are not meant to be understood as inherent qualities within Hashem, rather as the method of Hashem's activity, by which Hashem governs the world.

Rambam. *Moreh Nevuchim.* 1: 52.

According to many of the Mekubalim of Tzfas, (R. Eliyahu Di Vidas, R. Moshe *Alshich.* Bamidbar 14:20), simply reciting the Thirteen Attributes is not sufficient, one needs to embody and emulate these attributes in his relationships with others, and then they have power. The Ramak explains how we are to embody these qualities. The *Ma'or Va'shemesh* explains that this is the reason why we can only recite the Thirteen Attributes with a Minyan, a quorum of ten men, since if it is difficult for one person to always embody all these qualities, in the group, we can assume all these attributes are present. Yet, there are other sages who say that the way to activate the Attributes is simply by reciting them. *Safer Hafla'ah. Bnei Yissachar* Mamorei Elul. Maamor 2:4. Clearly, as the *Maharal* explains, for them to be effective we need to recite them with proper intention and focus.

Thirty-Two Gates *of* Wisdom
Awakening through Kabbalah

Kabbalah holds the secrets to a path of conscious awareness. In this compact book, renowned spiritual teacher Rav DovBer Pinson presents 32 key concepts of Kabbalah and shows their value in opening the gates of perception.

From the Introduction

Simply translated, Kabbalah means "that which is received." Looking deeper, the word Kabbalah can mean to be open and receptive, to challenge one's own internal navigational system in order to see, hear, and be open to... more.

We must be receptive to a teaching to fully absorb it. We turn ourselves into vessels and invite within that which we wish to understand or grasp. In this way, we become receptacles, dispensaries, and a part of the Kabbalah.

We become vessels of this tradition by opening the self to a higher reality, and viewing the spirit within the matter. We raise our consciousness to the point where the Divine within all creation is revealed. As we pursue a deeper awareness, we become less ego-centered and more attuned to the deeper

ABOUT THE AUTHOR

Rabbi DovBer Pinson is a world-renowned scholar, author, thinker, and beloved spiritual teacher. Through his books, lectures, and counsel he has touched and inspired the lives of thousands. Amongst his published works are: *Reincarnation & Judaism: The Journey of the Soul*; *Inner Rhythms: The Kabbalah of Music*; *Meditation & Judaism: Exploring Meditative Paths*; *Toward the Infinite: The Way of Kabbalistic Meditation*; *Jewish Wisdom of the Afterlife: The Myths, Mysteries & Meanings* and *Thirty-Two Gates of Wisdom: Awakening Through Kabbalah.*

Rav Pinson is an internationally acclaimed speaker and has lectured in both scholarly and lay settings throughout the globe. Rabbi Pinson is the Rosh Yeshiva of the IYYUN Yeshiva and heads IYYUN Center in Brownstone Brooklyn. More information is available at www.IYYUN.com

www.ingramcontent.com/pod-product-compliance
Ingram Content Group UK Ltd.
Pitfield, Milton Keynes, MK11 3LW, UK
UKHW041822200726
13854UKWH00001BA/443